DIVINITY AND ELECTRICITY

AF596096

- an analogy -

Décio Martins de Medeiros
São Paulo – Brasil

Copyright © 2024 Décio Martins de Medeiros

All rights reserved. No part of this work may be reproduced or used in any form or by any means, electronic or mechanical, including photocopying, recording, or by any information storage and retrieval system, without written permission, except for brief quotations in critical reviews or magazine articles. The author and the publisher are not responsible for any changes that may occur in the conventional or electronic addresses mentioned in this book.

This is a translation of the book 'Divindade e Eletricidade' published in Portuguese by Decio Martins de Medeiros.

Bibliographic Information:
Author: Decio Martins de Medeiros.
Title: Divinity and Electricity.
Subtitle: an analogy
Place, Year: São Paulo - Brazil, 2024.
Pages: 75 pages, 6"x9" size.
Subjects: 1. Divinity. 2. Christianity.

Table of Contents

The Divine Community 5
Different Analogies 7
Analogy with Electricity 9
The Divine Circuit 12
The Divine-Human Circuit 13
Human Resistance 35
Rising from the Dead 47
Divinity is Source AND Way AND Current of Gifts 58
The human person is an integrated body and soul. 63
About the Author 74

The Divine Community

Christians believe that the Divine is a community of three divine persons: The Divine Father, The Divine Son, and The Divine Holy Spirit.

These three divine persons are infinite, so the arithmetic of infinite numbers applies to them, not the arithmetic of finite numbers.

In finite arithmetic, if we add 1 finite to 1 finite to 1 finite, we get 3 finites. If we have 1 finite and divide it by 3, we get 1/3 finite.

In infinite arithmetic, if we add 1 infinite to 1 infinite to 1 infinite, we get 1 infinite. If we have 1 infinite and divide it by 3, we still get 1 infinite.

Adding infinites results in infinity.

Three Infinities equal One Infinity. Each of them is an infinite, and together they are one infinite. The Divine Father and the Divine Son are One Infinite. The Divine Father, the Divine Son, and the Divine Spirit are One Infinite.

Why only 1 Divine Father? Why only 1 Divine Son? Why only 1 Divine Spirit?

Because one divine source, one divine path, and one divine current are enough to transmit divinity through the heart of the human being.

The divine source is infinite, the divine path is infinite, the divine current is infinite, but the portion of divine current that passes through the heart of the human being is finite because the human being is finite. The amount of divine current that passes through the human heart depends on how much the person resists or opens up to receive it.

We need the three divine beings, the three individual infinities, each with the one and only infinite divine essence.

If there were only the Divine Father as the infinite source, it would be inaccessible and could not be dispensed to the human being.

For the Divine Father, the infinite source, to be accessible, we need the infinite path, the Divine Son. Starting from the infinite source, through the infinite path, the Divine Spirit, the infinite current, flows through the human being in the finite amount that the human allows and resists.

Different Analogies

It is intriguing to discover that some formulas linking quantities in the mechanical world have the same structure as those in the electrical world. Katsuhiko Ogata, in his book *Modern Control Engineering*, teaches us that:

"The concept of analogous systems is very useful in practice because one type of system may be easier to handle experimentally than another. For example, instead of building and studying a mechanical system, we can construct and study its electrical analogue because, in general, electrical or electronic systems are much easier to deal with."

"Analogies are not limited to electrical and mechanical systems; they are applicable to any systems as long as their differential equations, or transfer functions, are of identical form."

In the book *The Practice of Creativity*, the author George M. Prince teaches that, among the ways of thinking, the most constructive element is the use of metaphor, where a person draws an analogy between their problem and another object or idea. In Appendix 6 of his book, Prince offers a suggestion of worlds where we can seek to establish analogies with other worlds: Acoustics; Aeronautics; Agriculture; Animals; Archaeology; Architecture; Art; Astrophysics; Astronomy; Noise; Biology; Botany; Cinema; Comedy; Computers; Racing; Tribal customs; Criminology; Dance; Buildings; Education;

Electricity; Espionage; Sports; Exploration; Witchcraft; Science fiction; Philosophy; Finance; Physics; Geology; War; History; Machines; Mathematics; Medicine; Meteorology; Mineralogy; Mythology; Fashion; Models; Oceanography; Politics; Bridges; Chemistry; Rocks; Synthetic substances; Theater; Time and space; Woodworking; Metalworking; Transport; etc.

Analogy with Electricity

To understand the Divine, we can use the analogy of Electricity. In a simple electrical circuit with a power source, a conductor, a current, and a resistor, we can analogously consider the human being as the resistor, receiving the current of the Divine Holy Spirit. This current reaches the human being through Jesus Christ, the Divine Son, the incarnate divinity, who is the way to the source of everything, which is the Divine Father.

We will use our knowledge of electricity to seek a better understanding of divinity.

Both are invisible, but we can feel their effects.

Basic Concepts of Electricity:

- Electrical Power Source: An element with an electrical potential difference capable of providing an electric current through a circuit.

- Potential Difference: The difference in electric charge between the terminals of a power source.

- Electric Current: The flow of electrically charged particles through a conductor when there is a potential difference between the terminals.

- Electric Circuit: The path of the electric current generated by the source, passing through a conductor, through a load, and returning to the source.

- Electrical Resistance: An element with the physical capacity to oppose the flow of electric current even when there is an applied potential difference.

Christian Concepts of the Divine:

The Divine is a source of gifts for humanity. These gifts, originating from the Divine, need to pass through the divine-human interface to reach the person.

For the Christian:

- The Divine Father is the source of gifts.

- The Divine Holy Spirit is the bearer of the gifts that flow from the source.

- The Divine Son is the only interface between the divine and the human, the sole conductor of the bearer of the gifts from the source to the human being.

- A human being can be the recipient of the gifts if, by their own free will, they choose to accept or reject the gifts bestowed by the Divine.

The analogy we will use is:

- electrical source --- divine source

- electrical conductor --- divine conductor

- electrical current --- divine current

- resistance to electrical current --- resistance to divine current

The Divine Circuit

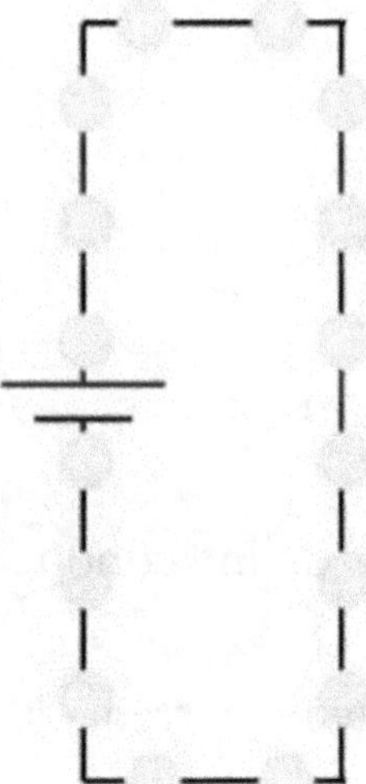

The divine circuit consists of a divine source, a divine conductor, and a divine current.

The divine current flows from the divine source, through the divine conductor, and returns to the divine source, which is not only a source but also a sink.

Divinity is the infinite source with an infinite conductor connecting its poles, through which an infinite current passes.

Divinity, without humanity, is a short circuit!

The Divine-Human Circuit

When we introduce the human race into this circuit, it acts as a resistance to the flow of the divine current.

The divine conductor that connects the poles of the divine source is the same one that links the poles of humanity. It is Christ, the incarnate divinity, the divine-human conductor, the interface between divinity and humanity. The intensity of the current that flows from the source, travels through the conductor, and then passes through the human person depends on the resistance that the human person exerts.

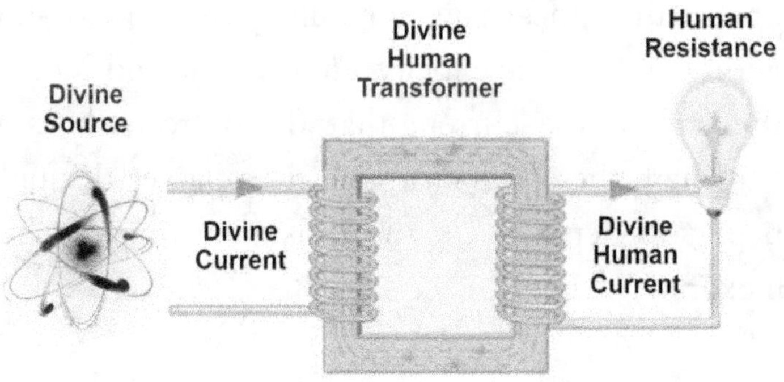

Christ, who is the incarnate divinity, is both human and divine, the divine-human interface, the conductor that allows the divine current, originating from the divine source and flowing through the divine conductor, to pass through the human race and return to the divine source.

The substance of divinity is spiritual.

The divine source produces a spiritual divine current, the very substance of divinity.

The Divine Spirit is what the Divinity dispenses to human beings.

It is through the divine circuit (source, conductor, current) that the divine spiritual current is dispensed to human beings.

The love of the divine source, the grace of the divine conductor, and the communion of the divine current are the three stages of the one Divinity.

Without these three stages, the essence of Divinity, that is, the divine spiritual current, could never be dispensed to human beings.

The Divine circuit is developed from the Divine source, in the Divine conductor, and through the Divine current.

The divine source is the origin of all things visible and invisible.

The divine source is invisible and unreachable.

The divinity incarnate in Christ, the divine conductor, the divine-human interface, is accessible to humanity.

All the fullness of the divine source passes through the divine conductor.

The invisible divine source is revealed in Christ, the incarnate divinity, the divine conductor, who is the image, the expression of Divinity.

The divine source and the divine conductor are one divine circuit.

Through the divine conductor, the inaccessible divine source becomes accessible to human beings.

Thus, the human person can interact with the divine source through the divine conductor.

Christ, the incarnate divinity, is the divine conductor. He is the divine-human interface.

The divinity passes through human beings by means of the divine current that comes from the divine source and is transmitted to humans by the divine conductor.

The divine current carries with it the divinity of the source and the human touch of the conductor, who is both divine and human.

Christ, the divine conductor, is the incarnation of divinity. The divine current is the perception of Christ.

The divine current gives life to the human being.

Through the divine current, the human person contacts divinity and experiences Christ.

The divine source, the divine conductor, and the divine current are not three divinities but one Divinity.

The divinity of the source is in the incarnate divine conductor, and the divine conductor, with his divine-human interface, transmits the divinity in the divine current.

When the divine current enters the human person, it is the very divinity of the divine source that is dispensed to the human person.

The purpose of the divine circuit is to dispense divinity to the human spirit. Thus, divinity dwells in the human spirit. The human person is a temple of divinity.

The divine source, the divine conductor, and the divine current may seem like three different types of divinity, but in reality, they are one divinity.

If divinity did not exist, there would be no divine source, no divine conductor, and no divine current.

At one end of the divine-human circuit is the divine source, the reservoir of divinity, while at the other end is humanity. Between the two ends is Christ, the incarnate divinity, the divine conductor, the interface between the divine and the human. Through this circuit flows the divine current.

Everything that the divine source and the divine conductor are and everything they have is in the divine current.

The divine current comes to us through the divine and human nature of Christ, the incarnate divinity, the divine-human conductor.

The divine current provides guidance to the human person. The intensity of the divine current passing through the human person is greater the less resistance the person offers to its passage and the more it is enjoyed by the human person.

The fundamental point of the divine circuit connected to humanity is the divine current dwelling in our human spirit.

The human person needs to learn not to resist the passage of the divine current. To learn to have communion with Christ, the incarnate divinity, the divine conductor.

The human person needs to deal with the divine current that passes through them, for it is the nourishment that comes from divinity.

The fundamental point of the divine-human circuit is to deal with Christ, the incarnate divinity, the divine conductor, to receive the divine current and be filled with it.

The fundamental point of the divine-human circuit is the divine source expressed in the divine conductor, the divine conductor expressed in the divine current, and the divine current expressed in us.

When we come into contact with Christ, the incarnate divinity, the conductor of the divine current, this current will then dispense life into us, bringing inner illumination.

The divine current transmits life to us, liberates, and transforms our inner nature and outer form.

The divine current renews our mind, emotions, and will.

Human beings are a resistance to the flow of the electric current.

The human being has their human spirit at the center of their soul.

It is through the human spirit that the divine current flows.

Our human spirit is the dwelling place of the divine current. Divinity is accessible to the human being because it dwells in our spirit.

If our soul prevents the flow of the divine current, we will not be able to come into contact with the divinity.

The divine current must penetrate our soul in such a way as to enter our spirit.

The first gift of every Christian existence, the fundamental gift, is the divine current. The divine current is the gift Jesus promised to send us. Without the divine current, there is no relationship with Christ, the divine conductor, nor with the divine source. For the divine current opens our hearts to the presence of divinity and draws it toward the source of love that is the divine source.

Christ, the incarnate divine conductor, must touch us in such a way as to allow the divine current to flow through our human spirit.

The divinity, through the divine current, takes our human spirit as its dwelling place. We must forget everything and focus on Christ, the divine conductor who, through his divine current, dwells within our human spirit.

The will of the divinity is that the human person turns inward to their human spirit, where they can contact the divine current, be filled with the divine current, occupied by the divine current, and be one with the divine current. The human person must allow the divine current, which dwells in their human spirit, to take control and possession of them.

We pray that the divine current reaches us so that we may be nourished by its energy.

If we are believers, then we have the divine current flowing through our human spirit.

When our human spirit is repentant before the divinity and open to it, it does not resist the flow of the divine current.

The gifts we receive are a help, but they are not the goal or the crucial point. The crucial point is Christ, who conducts the divine current, who dwells within the spirit of the person. The divinity is the source of love, and love is the expression of life.

In order not to resist the flow of the divine current, we must seek to escape our thoughts, emotions, and choices, and thus, emptying ourselves, make room for the divine current to fill our human spirit.

Christian meditation is a practice with this purpose, inviting the divine current to visit our human spirit by silently repeating the Aramaic words *Maranatha*, which means 'Come, Lord.'

The divine current that overcomes human resistance is what gives life, revives, and strengthens the person in their integrity of body and soul and in their innermost part, their human spirit.

The human spirit is the dwelling place of the divine current and is intertwined with it.

The human spirit is the place where we can experience the divine current. Our human spirit is the place to receive the divine current.

The goal of divinity is to dispense its divine current to the human being, and the place where this happens is in the human spirit.

No effort is needed, only not to resist the flow of the divine current. The flow of the divine current will bear fruit in the person.

The gifts result from the divine current experienced as grace by the person. A person may receive spiritual gifts and still remain carnal and immature. The person must focus on turning inward, to their human spirit, to their core, to contact the divine current and commune with it. This should be a constant exercise, and this exercise is the key to a life of communion with the divinity that dwells within us.

In the divine circuit, the source is invisible, the current is invisible, but the conductor, the human-divine interface, the human-divine transformer, is visible. The divine current shines in our core, the innermost part of our soul, for the illumination of the knowledge of the glory of the divine source, expressed by the conductor, the human-divine interface.

Lamps are needed to "contain" electricity. Humanity was created to "contain" divinity, so that divinity could express itself through its creatures. Human beings were made to be the temple of the divine current. The human being is the vessel created to receive the divine current, with its content of love that comes from the divine source, through the divine conductor (the human-divine transformer interface) and reaches the innermost part, the core of the human person.

Divinity is a source of gifts for humanity. The greatest gift is the divine current that passes through the innermost part of the human person. This divine current, which comes from the divine source, reaches the human person, conducted by the human-divine interface, the human-divine transformer: Christ. All gifts received by the human person are fruits of the divine current that passes through their innermost being.

The divine source, the divine-human transforming conductor, and the divine current are one divine circuit, one divinity. It is through the three distinct elements of the divine circuit that the divinity executes its will of bringing the divine current into the human person. The will of the divinity is to express itself in each human person through its three divine elements: the source, the divine-human transforming conductor, and the current, forming one single divine circuit.

And the human circuit? What are its elements? Body, soul (mind), and spirit (heart, core, innermost center of the soul). We need to adjust our mind and heart so that, through the understanding of the mind and the receptiveness of the heart, we can receive the divine current. In some people, the mind is closed, or the heart is closed, and thus they do not have the opportunity to experience the divine current. To experience the divine current, we need to deal with our mind and properly tune our heart, thus fulfilling the will of the divinity.

The parts of the soul are mind, will, and emotion. The parts of the human spirit are conscience, communion, and intuition. The innermost part of the person, their core, their heart, includes the mind, will, emotion, and conscience. The function of the human spirit is to come into contact with the divine current, to commune with the divinity, to receive it and worship it. When the divine current touches our human spirit, it is revived. The divine current gives life, energizes our human spirit.

The human person must frequently invoke the word Maranatha (which means, come, divinity), so that the divine current may come, and with it, its good and creative force, enabling them to be less selfish and more altruistic, becoming a sign of comfort and hope to others. The presence of the divine current flowing through the human spirit makes them capable of perceiving the presence of the divinity and its work, not in great things but in the small ones.

The human spirit is not only revived but also receives another life into it. This other life is the divine current. When the divine current comes into the human spirit, it not only gives life to our dead spirit but also introduces the very divinity into our spirit. This is regeneration, the new life, where the human spirit is merged with the divine spirit.

The electric lamp is a good analogy to represent the human being in contact with divinity.

The lamp has a part that can come into contact with electricity. The human being has the human spirit, which can come into contact with divinity.

When the lamp connects to the electric current, it produces heat in its body and illuminates both its interior and exterior. When the human spirit is connected to the divine current, it energizes the human body and illuminates the soul, which then reflects outward.

The body of the lamp protects its internal parts, just as the human body protects its inner parts. A human being is like a lamp that, when the divine current flows through it, ignites its spirit, enlivens its soul, and gives life to its body! The divine conductor, the interface between the divine and human transformer, is the light of the world.

The divine current, when sought and received by a person, can relax the body, calm the mind, and bring peace to the heart.

This wonderful divine current resides within our human spirit. Our human spirit, blended with the divine current, forms one single spirit. The human spirit is the core, the innermost part of the human being, and its role is to contact and experience divinity.

After the human spirit is animated by the passage of the divine current and becomes united with it as one single current, one single spirit, then the human spirit becomes capable of interacting with divinity.

The first thing we need to learn to reduce human resistance to the flow of the divine current is to deny our soul, which is our ego.

Since the soul consists of three parts (mind, will, emotion), in order to reduce human resistance to the divine current, we must learn to deny our natural mind, our natural will, and our natural emotions.

Secondly, the soul needs to be purified by receiving the current of divinity. The more we deny our soul, our ego, the more it will be purified by divinity.

Thirdly, our soul needs to be transformed. The soul must be denied, then purified, and finally transformed in order to reflect divinity.

Our relationship with divinity is always initiated and sustained by our innermost being, by our human spirit.

Anything that enters our human spirit must pass through our soul, and anything that comes out of our human spirit must pass through our soul.

Thus, our soul has the power to open or close the innermost part, the core, the heart of the human being.

The most effective way to open people's hearts is to communicate the love of divinity.

When the doors of the heart are fully opened, it becomes easy for the divine current to touch the human spirit.

If a person is full of themselves, they are closed off to the entry of the divine current. They need to empty their human spirit in order to open up and receive the divine current.

When the heart is open, the conscience becomes more sensitive.

A heavy conscience acts as resistance to our contact with the divine current.

Repenting and confessing our faults clears our conscience.

If the conscience is heavy, there is no contact with the divine current, intuition doesn't function, and our human spirit does not feel the desire to receive divinity.

When the divine current touches our human spirit, we gain an inner knowledge, we sense something of divinity in our human spirit, and we need the mind to comprehend what we feel in our human spirit.

With the passage of the divine current through the human spirit, we have eternal life, and it must spread into the innermost parts of the soul and saturate them with itself. This will transform the human soul into the divine image. The image of Christ will then be reflected in the person's thoughts. The mind will understand what the person feels in their human spirit.

The mind will no longer act on its own but will be placed in the human spirit, which is traversed by the divine current. The mind will be set on the spiritual part and not on the material body.

The more the mind remains with the divine current flowing through the human spirit, the more it will be under the control of that spirit.

But only when, by our own will, we are ready to obey the divine will, will we be able to understand.

The divinity created humans with free will and always leaves humans the choice.

How can the flow of the divine current enter the innermost parts of the human person?

Christ accomplished His work on the cross and thus introduced the divine current flowing within us.

But why then do so many people not experience the free flow of the divine current?

Because the flow of spiritual life, the flow of the divine current, is not released inside those people.

There is much filth that needs to be removed—filth in their conscience, emotions, will, and mind.

To reduce resistance to the flow of the divine current, a person must want to cleanse their heart, their human spirit. They must repent of their mistakes and ask for forgiveness.

To reduce the resistance to the passage of the divine current, a person must deny their ego, stop being full of themselves, and make room for the flow of the divine current.

To understand how the divine current transforms us, we must first understand what the divine current is.

Human beings are incomplete without the divine current.

The divinity has made its divine current available to those who accept it in their hearts, in their core, in their innermost being, in their human spirit.

The scriptures portray the divine current as the manifestation of the power of the divinity in His creation.

The divinity can infuse us with divine gifts. These divine spiritual attributes transform our human nature as we become participants in the divine nature. By making this right choice, we must then use the divine current to overcome our carnal nature.

Just as electrical current is essential to light a lamp, so too the divine current is essential for eternal life. And just as electrical current is an invisible and powerful force, so too is the divine current an invisible and powerful force for our spiritual growth.

The divine current can be compared to an electrical current. Electricity flows through a conductor connected to its source to operate a device. As long as the flow of electrical current from that source remains uninterrupted, the device has full power. But any interruption in electrical current comes with a loss of energy to that device. Permanent contact with this source of electrical power is essential.

The same happens with the divine current. Since humans do not have the ability to store the divine current to use at will, if we sever our relationship with the divinity, we distance ourselves from this power that acts within us. That is why our inner being, our human spirit, must be renewed day by day.

How can the divine current be a gift if its effect on us depends on maintaining a constant relationship with the divinity?

The divine current as a gift is only available to those who live within the limits set by the divinity.

Maintaining a close relationship with the divinity is the key to receiving His divine current. The divinity is the source of this divine current that reaches us through the divine-human interface, which is the divine conductor, a divine-human transformer.

The divinity, actively and directly, empowers us through His divine current.

The divine current, as our helper, implies a source of aid that is available in our moments of difficulty or concern—transmitting to us the guidance and assistance of the divinity.

The divinity is in heaven, but at the same time, He is within us, just as the electricity at the source is the same as the one in our home.

To use electricity at home, we need to flip the switch; in the same way, to experience divinity, a person needs to flip the switch, which is the human spirit, and thus the divine current flows through the human spirit.
Although the divine current flows through our human spirit, it is closely connected to our soul.
The divine current is in our human spirit, but the way to reach it is by ceasing to be full of oneself, day after day.
The soul is the ego. The ego is the very center of the human person, and it is the ego that needs to be nullified.
Many people often use the word 'I.' In these people, there is nothing but ego, being full of oneself. For the Christian, life should be about emptying oneself. Stop saying 'I, I, I,' and more of 'Christ who lives in each of us.'
Denying the soul means shifting focus from oneself to the human spirit, where the divine current flows, laden with gifts.
All a person's needs are met in the divine current that flows through their human spirit.
When we allow the divine current to flow through our human spirit, it can fill and occupy us.
The divine current carries gifts to our spirit so that we may bear fruit.
Where is the key to contact divinity?
It is in our human spirit.
The divinity, which is unlimited, limited itself to dwell in our human spirit.
Therefore, we need to learn how to flip the switch to connect with divinity.
At every moment, we must turn back to our self, which is in our human spirit, disconnecting from our ego that is in our mind, in our soul.

We must forget the things around us and enjoy the divine current that flows through our human spirit.
Inner peace will be reflected outward.
When you are in a difficult situation, turn to your human spirit and contact the divinity.
Whenever we turn to our human spirit to contact the divine current, we are in the light, in communion with divinity. Exercising the human spirit and denying the life of the mind, the life of the soul.
The divinity created the human being as the center of all creation with the purpose of expressing itself.
The human being has divine and eternal life, which is the very divinity as our life.
The difference between divinity and divine life is like the difference between electricity and light.
Electricity is used not only as light but also as power, heat, etc.
In the same way, divinity is our life and many other things.
The divine current in our human spirit is eternal life. If the human spirit does not contain the divine current, then there is no eternal life, because eternal life is in the divine current.
The human person does not gain eternal life when they rise from the dead; they rise from the dead because they have the divine current in their human spirit.
It is through the flow of the divine current that all the riches of divinity are brought to us.
The more we have the flow of the divine current, the more we will be in the presence of divinity, and thus we will know the will and the way of divinity.

Human Resistance

The matter from which human beings are made has existed for millions of years, but the history of the spiritual dimension of life, as recorded by writing, is only a few thousand years old. The material dimension of life is the visible part, the object of scientific study. Science continues its search for more knowledge and, in doing so, encounters more and more of the unknown: Newton published his laws of motion, Maxwell's thermodynamics made Newton's laws insufficient, Einstein declared Newton's hypothesis about time false, and quantum physics showed that Newton's laws do not apply to the world of small particles. String theory showed that quantum physics is incomplete, and M-theory revealed that string theory itself is incomplete. M-theory, which is an extension of string theory, still needs empirical corroboration… and we are now at the limits of our mathematics. This field needs to evolve to support the new physics that is emerging. What is missing to complete these theories? There will always be something missing… The human being is limited, but the unknown is unlimited!

Science recognizes that it doesn't have all the answers to life's mysteries. The more science discovers, the more it wants and needs to discover. The more questions are answered, the greater the number of questions to be addressed. Ultimately, it is discovered that the "size" of the unknown is infinitely greater than what has become known. At first, little is known, and one is unaware of how much is yet to be known. As more is learned, it becomes clear that there is far more to discover. In the end, it is understood that the size of the unknown is infinitely greater than the size of the known.

The spiritual dimension of life is invisible, immaterial, known to some mystics and religious individuals, unknown to many, and nonexistent to others. Science works with the material dimension and has no means of proving that the spiritual dimension does not exist.

Science and reason can only grasp what is of a tangible nature, while the intelligence of the heart is capable of grasping suprasensible principles. The pressing question: What causes chemistry to turn into biology? The material and spiritual dimensions are distinct, yet interrelated, and they integrate the person as a whole.

When a person is born, they come programmed with a unique and individual personality, some knowledge, and certain talents, carried as genetic memory. Additional knowledge can be acquired through science and can also be discovered by chance, as if by revelation or insight. On the other hand, humans encounter the unknown when they are born, when they live, and when they die. The knowledge gained from discoveries of what was once unknown is as though the unknown itself creates the known.

Just as a computer has a material dimension, the hardware, and a non-material dimension, the software, and requires energy to function, so too does the human person. The human being has a material dimension, the physical dimension, and a non-physical dimension, the spiritual dimension, and requires vital energy to function. Just as a computer leaves the factory loaded with an operating system and some basic applications, and over time acquires new ones, the same happens with the human person.

The "applications" of the spiritual dimension of the human person are: mind, will, emotion, conscience, intuition, and companionship. The spiritual dimension encompasses appreciating good music, admiring a beautiful painting, singing a song, crying, feeling emotion, loving, believing, experiencing relationships with others, detaching from a situation, surprises, whims, luck, or misfortune. The software "animates" the hardware. The spiritual dimension "animates" the physical dimension.

The physical bodies of all people are made up of the same chemical elements. What makes each person unique and unrepeatable lies in their spiritual dimension, which gives a unique form to their physical body.

At the center, at the core, in the innermost part of a person's spiritual dimension lies the essence of the person. Notice that the essence of a person does not change even when all the atoms in their body, their thoughts, their emotions, their achievements, their relationships, and their possessions change. A person may lose all their possessions, yet their essence remains the same, the same person.

In the spiritual dimension of a person, in their "operating system," there is something that drives them to seek light, truth, and the unknown. As we draw closer to the light, to the truth, we "see" with more clarity. The further we move away from the light, from the truth, the less we "see." I have personally experienced this: the more I distanced myself from the Light, the more things became nebulous, confusing, and I wasn't even aware that I was heading in the wrong direction, away from the Light. The closer I come to the Light, the clearer everything becomes.

The more a creature is allowed to approach the unknown, the more reverence they feel towards it.

The main cause of human resistance to the flow of the divine current is the ego.

How can we reduce resistance and make space in our hearts to receive the divine and hidden Friend?

The answer is to continually recite the Christian mantra. Call upon the Lord with the mantra *Maranatha!*

The repetition of the *Maranatha* mantra leads the person beyond their ego.

When repeating the mantra, the ego resists because, being full of itself, it doesn't want to make any space in the heart, thus creating resistance.

This resistance is instinctive, as the ego fears losing ground or diminishing its influence.

We must say the mantra continuously to bring the ego under our control.

An uncontrolled ego is the source of suffering, anger, and violence.

A controlled ego is happier.

Contemplation, meditation, and pure observation, without analysis, reduce human resistance to the flow of the divine current.

Observing without analyzing, without judging, just observing, helps to separate the true "self" from the "ego"; that is, it helps to discern and distinguish the "human spirit" from the "soul," thus reducing human resistance to the divine current, which is the Holy Spirit, allowing it to merge with our human spirit, forming one spirit in our heart, at our core—at the innermost part of our soul, of our being.

The practice of contemplation, such as contemplating the nature of plants, animals, people, and oneself, and maintaining peace in the heart with the acceptance of life as it is, opens our spirit to the coming of the Holy Spirit into our heart.

Feeling peace in the heart is experiencing the presence of the Holy Spirit.

Anthony de Mello teaches that self-observation is observing everything in you and around you, as distantly as possible, as if you were another person. This is not the same as self-absorption or self-concern.

He recommends facing things as if you had no connection with them. Be a passive observer, don't interfere, watch, observe, don't try to change anything, don't judge, don't take action. Eliminate the ideas of good and evil, stop all judgments, just observe.

Awareness is understanding that what you call the Self is nothing more than the sum of your past experiences, your conditioning, your programming. The Self is not your thoughts, your body, your name, your career, your beliefs, or your religion. The Self is not your labels. Labels belong to the Ego. What constantly changes is the Ego. The Self never changes. The Self is the observer.

He states that being aware of reality means observing, seeing things, discarding illusions and fantasies, and beginning to come into contact with the facts.

Once you understand what the Self is, nothing will hurt you because no one can reach your Self; they can only affect your Ego.

When anxiety comes, don't fight it, just observe it and let it pass.

The author teaches that the reason you're not feeling joyful right now is that you're thinking about what you don't have. Focus on the present and be happy.

To disconnect from your Ego, observe everything as if it were happening to someone else: without comments, without judgment, without interference, without trying to change anything, just understanding.

In self-observation, take notice of what you are saying, doing, thinking, acting upon. Become aware of the reasons behind these actions. You control what you are conscious of; what you are not conscious of controls you.

Consciousness is not concentration. Concentration is focus. Consciousness is being open to anything that enters your field of action.

To find your true Self, free yourself from labels and the Ego. Worrying about your labels invites suffering. Suffering is a sign that you are not in touch with the truth. When you are conscious, you have no worries; you are happy!

Those who are not conscious are manipulated, do not enjoy life, and are always tense and anxious. This happens because they are identifying with one of their labels—money, job, profession.

Your essential Self is not your profession, your clothes, your name. The Ego is all of your labels.

Four steps to wisdom:

1. Be aware of the negative feelings within you.

2. Understand that these feelings are within you and not part of the external reality.

3. Never identify with these feelings, for they have nothing to do with your true Self. Feelings come and go.

4. Don't try to change things! No! Change yourself! Understand that when you transform, everything transforms.

With consciousness, you won't try to change the world. With consciousness, you'll know what to do or what not to do.

What should you do to transform yourself? All you need to do is understand. Think of someone who puts you in a bad mood. Understand that this negative feeling is inside you. You are responsible for this feeling, not the other person. Someone else might feel good in that person's presence. Do not make demands or have expectations of the person. Free the tyrant within you. Don't tell the person what they should be or how they should behave.

Saying no to people is part of the awareness that you live your life the way you want, and that is not selfishness. Selfishness is demanding that others live their lives the way you want them to. You should not demand anything from anyone for your own well-being.

As consciousness grows, you react less and act more.

Every time you feel unhappy, it is because you have added something to reality. Reality provides the stimulus, and you provide the reaction. This addition is an illusion. The illusion is thinking that by changing the external world, you will change yourself. No, you will not! You have to flow with life. What makes you happy is being in touch with reality at every moment. Neither people nor external events have the power to hurt you; you give them that power.

You need to be conscious of your prejudices, your likes, your dislikes, and your preferences. If what you experience is your concept or prejudice, then you are not experiencing reality because reality is concrete. A concept is static, while reality is dynamic.

Anthony de Mello's proposal is to bring you to an awareness of the reality around you. Consciousness means observing—observing what is happening within you and around you. Look, observe, spend hours watching people, trees, birds, stones, and grass. See the reality that is beyond words and concepts. Let go of your concepts, let go of your opinions, let go of your prejudices, let go of your judgments.

When you turn on the light of consciousness, darkness disappears.

Until you are conscious of yourself, you have no right to interfere with the world or anyone in it.

For self-transformation, you need:

1. Inner vision (without effort, without cultivating habits, without having an ideal).

2. Understanding.

3. Consciousness.

An Eastern proverb: "If the eye is unobstructed, the result is vision; if the ear is unobstructed, the result is hearing; if the nose is unobstructed, the result is smell; if the mouth is unobstructed, the result is taste; if the mind is unobstructed, the result is wisdom."

Reality is perceived when you eliminate your concepts and conditioning.

In summary: The true Self is the observer, the one who sees, residing at your core, in your heart, in your human spirit.

The Ego is what you think you are, dwelling in your mind, in your soul.

The whole human being is body, soul, and human spirit—all united, inseparable.

Rising from the Dead

If the human being is an integral being of body (form) + soul (mind) + spirit.

If with the incarnation of the Divine Son, Christ has both divine and human nature.

If the will of the Divine Father is that Christ be the way to send the Divine Spirit to the human spirit of all people.

If the Divine Spirit and the human spirit blend into one divine and human spirit.

Then, through Christ, with Christ, and in Christ, all of humankind has within its human spirit the very divinity.

As the divinity dwells in the human spirit, the integral human being is inhabited by divinity.

The divinity that inhabits the integral human being is what causes them to rise from the dead, integrally: body + soul + spirit.

The Resurrected Body According to Some Translations of 1 Corinthians 15:42-44

A Catholic Christian translation: The integral human being, before resurrection, is body integrated with soul, and after resurrection continues to be an integral human being, but becomes body integrated with spirit:

"It is the same with the resurrection of the dead: the thing that is sown is perishable but what is raised is imperishable; the thing that is sown is contemptible but what is raised is glorious; the thing that is sown is weak but what's raised is powerful; when it is sown it embodies the soul, when it is raised it embodies the spirit. If the soul has its own embodiment, so does the spirit have its own embodiment."

The Jerusalem Bible in English at www.unz.org/Pub/Bible-1966v02-00292

In the Jerusalem Bible in Portuguese we have:

"The same is true for the resurrection of the dead; sown corruptible, the body rises incorruptible; sown in dishonor, it rises shining with glory; sown in weakness, it rises full of strength; sown a natural body, it rises a spiritual body. If there is a natural body, there is also a spiritual body."

In note G of the Jerusalem Bible in Portuguese, printed by Paulus in 2002, it explains that the psychic body is the human body animated by the psyché (Heb. nefesh), the living soul. From 'psychic' the body will become 'pneumatic', incorruptible, immortal, glorious, freed from the laws of earthly matter and its appearances.

A Messianic Jewish translation: The integral human being after resurrection will be a body controlled by the Holy Spirit:

"Thus is it with the resurrection of the dead. When the body is sown, it suffers decomposition; upon being resurrected, it will never decompose again. When sown, it lacks dignity; upon rising, it will be wonderful. When sown, it is weak; when it rises, it will be strong. When sown, it is a common human body; when it rises, it will be a body controlled by the Spirit. If there is a common human body, there is also a body controlled by the Spirit."

Complete Jewish Bible translated by David H. Stern published by Vida in 2011

A Protestant Christian translation: The integral human being after resurrection has a body related to the body before resurrection but different in essence.

"For so also is the resurrection of the dead. It is sown in corruption, it is raised in incorruption. It is sown in dishonor, it is raised in glory. It is sown in weakness, it is raised in power. It is sown a natural body, it is raised a spiritual body. If there is a natural body, there is also a spiritual body."

Expanded Annotated Bible, Charles C. Ryrie, Christian World Publishing, 2007

In the commentary on 1 Corinthians 15:35-50, the translator states, "In this passage, Paul explains that this is the body that the divinity chose to give to the resurrected (v.38), related to the first (v.36), but different in its essence (v.39-41)."

In the commentary on 1 Corinthians 15:49, the translator states that the resurrected body will be similar to that of Christ.

....

According to Renold J. Blank's perspective in his book *Eschatology of the Person*, published by Paulus in 2000:

p. 109: "THE RESURRECTION OCCURS AT DEATH:

The soul of a human being never separates from the body because it forms an indivisible unit of the unique and substantial human person.

This person, at death, enters a new timeless dimension called eternity.

At that moment, time ceases to exist as an existential dimension for this person. For them, death means 'the end of times.'

Since there is no time, there can be no passage of time between one event and another. Because of this, it is impossible for a soul to be separated from the body in eternity, waiting there for the resurrection of the body. In a timeless dimension, nothing can be awaited, as this dimension is the atemporal now.

The soul of a person who dies no longer has time to separate from the body, for the simple fact that time no longer exists.

The moment of death and the moment of the End of Times coincide in eternity.

However, at the End of Times, the resurrection of the body occurs, as the Church has always and justifiably declared.

Since this End of Times happens at the moment of death, it is also at this same moment that the resurrection of the body must necessarily occur.

Never, at any moment, does the human soul separate from the body and remain alone; this is simply because this soul, between death and the End of Times, would not even have time to separate from the body, because, in eternity, time no longer exists.

Based on these logical reflections and considering the non-dualistic biblical model of man, contemporary eschatology has formulated a new model, where attempts are made to overcome the contradictions of the previous model:

THE RESURRECTION OF THE HUMAN PERSON IN BODY AND SOUL OCCURS AT THE MOMENT OF THEIR DEATH, WHEN THIS WHOLE AND INTEGRAL PERSON LEAVES THEIR CONNECTION TO TIME AND ENTERS A NEW DIMENSION CALLED ETERNITY.

The death of this human person does not signify annihilation but a profound transformation of their entire being (cf. Paul: 1 Cor 15). The agent of this transformation is the divinity. This divinity does not transform only a part of man but the entire person. It maintains and preserves the total and global identity of what this person is, in all their dimensions, in such a way that, in this transformation, "the person reaches their full personal identity." This is what the biblical texts express through the formula of the resurrection of the dead. Throughout all ages and against all Gnostic and dualistic temptations, the Church has always remained firm in this faith."

p. 148: “AT DEATH, THE IDENTITY OF THE PERSON IS PRESERVED, AND FOR THE FIRST TIME, THIS PERSON KNOWS THEMSELVES IN ALL THEIR DIMENSIONS.

All the images used to explain the transformation that the human being undergoes at death make it very clear a fundamental fact: what is being transformed is the outer form, that which we call the body.

What, however, remains throughout this transformation is the identity of the person as a psychomaterial being. The person remains the same. They are identical to the person who died, with the same character, with the same characteristics, with all their dimensions, including the material dimensions. The resurrected person is a formed and defined self.

The structure of this “self,” however, has formed in such a way during life that we can say that, at death, the person is exactly that person, that personality they themselves constructed during their life.”

"In light of this fact—and after reflecting on the transformation of the bodily dimension in the resurrection—we must now ask what happens to this person formed when they died. In this reflection, we must always keep in mind that what we reflect upon here, in successive steps, is actually a single process, a single global and integral event that the human being undergoes in death and which we call resurrection."

"In my view, based on the study of Christian Eschatology books and the revelation of the apostle Paul in chapter 15 of the first letter to the Corinthians, we will rise from death in our same body but now with celestial matter and controlled by the Holy Spirit.

When the body dies on Earth, then the earthly matter of that body begins to decompose rapidly, and in the blink of an eye, the body rises in Heaven with celestial matter.

Verses 20 to 22 allow us to hope that, when we die on Earth, we will rise in Heaven, for it was so with Jesus Christ, and thus we hope it will be with us.

Verse 40 reveals that there are earthly bodies and celestial bodies.

Verse 42 reveals that the body with earthly matter undergoes decomposition. The body with celestial matter does not undergo decomposition.

Verse 44 is key to understanding the type of our celestial body. According to the site [Biblical Library](https://bibliotecabiblica.blogspot.com/2015/09/significado-de-1-corintios-15.html), 15:44-49—Animal [...] spiritual. The contrast is not between a material body and an immaterial one, but between that which is subject to death and that which is immortal. The Greek term translated as spiritual here refers to a body controlled by the Spirit, as opposed to one dominated by the flesh (1 Co 2:15; 10:4). The first man [...] the second man contrasts the sinful nature that every person inherits with the new and justified nature that we obtain through Christ.

Verse 48 reveals to us that people born of the earth are similar to the man of the earth (Adam). People born of Heaven are like the man of Heaven (Jesus Christ).

According to the site [Biblical Library](https://bibliotecabiblica.blogspot.com/2015/09/s

ignificado-de-1-corintios-15.html), 15:50—Flesh and blood cannot enter the glorious existence of an immortal body (vv. 35-49). Something must happen to this flesh for it to become incorruptible (v. 42).

Verses 51 and 52 reveal to us that in the end times, we will all be changed in an instant, in the blink of an eye.

Verse 52 reveals that in the end times, the dead will rise to live forever.

What happens at the end of times for a person?

After crossing the boundary, there is no longer the counting of time as we know it.

How does the passage of a person happen?

In the blink of an eye, the earthly material body transforms into a celestial spiritual body. The matter decomposes. Before and after the passage, the soul, which has always been spiritual, remains integrated with the body. The human being is an integrated body and soul being. Before the passage, the human being is an integrated material body and spiritual soul. After the passage, the human being is an integrated spiritual body and spiritual soul.

What does a person take to their resurrection?

In the resurrection, a person has everything that is unique and exclusive to them: their proper name, the names of their ancestors, their identity, their fingerprint, their DNA, their genetic memory, the shape of their body, their life history, their social relationships, their conscious and unconscious psychic memory, their talents, their personality, and their temperament.

For the believer, death is the passage to eternal life; it is a gain because they will be with Christ. According to Paul's Letter to the Philippians, Chapter 1, Verses 21 to 23."

....

Divinity is Source AND Way AND Current of Gifts

This is a Christian reflection on the divine circuit of gifts. John, the disciple, apostle, and contemporary of Christ, revealed that Divinity is love. Check in the First Epistle of John, chapter 4, verses 8 and 16. The Divine Father is the source of infinite love. Christ is the way of love that comes from the Father. Check in John 14:6. Jesus Christ revealed that the Father and He are one. Check in John 10:30. The Divine Father and the Divine Son are a circuit through which the current of infinite love flows.

Human beings are granted participation, through Christ, in the current of love that flows in the circuit of infinite love. John Main, a Benedictine monk and leader of the World Community for Christian Meditation, in his book on meditation titled *The Way of Unknowing*, in the chapter 'The Barrier of Distractions,' teaches that "The extraordinary truth about the Christian proclamation is that each and every one of us, regardless of our starting point, is invited to open our consciousness completely to the consciousness of Jesus, and in this opening, to be led out of ourselves, beyond ourselves, toward that conscious current of love that flows between Jesus and the Father."

In summary:

Divinity is a Circuit of Infinite Love with 3 Infinite Elements: a Source of Infinite Love; a Way of Infinite Love; a Current of Infinite Love.

The Way of Infinite Love has zero resistance to the passage of the Current of Infinite Love that comes from the Source and passes through the Way.

Humans are capable of receiving a finite portion of the Current of Love since humans have some resistance to the passage of the Current.

To dispense itself to human beings, Divinity utilizes the three divine persons: the Divine Father as the source, the Divine Incarnate Son as the transmission line, and the Divine Spirit as the current.

The Divine Spirit dwelling in the human spirit to dispense to humans everything that divinity is in Christ is the purpose of divinity. The Divine Spirit is what divinity dispenses to humans. The Apostle Paul says in 2 Corinthians 13:13: "The grace of the Lord Jesus Christ, the love of God, and the communion of the Holy Spirit be with you all!"

Love, grace, and communion are a single element in three stages: love is the source, grace is the expression of love, and communion is the transmission of that love in grace. The Divine Father, the Divine Son, and the Divine Spirit are a single divinity expressed in three Persons: The Divine Father is the source, the Divine Son is the expression of the Divine Father, and the Divine Spirit is the current transmitted to humans, bringing divinity in Christ into the human being. Without these three stages, the essence of divinity could not be dispensed to humans. The action of divinity is developed from the Divine Father, in the Divine Son, and through the Divine Spirit.

The Divine Father is the universal source of all things. He is invisible and unattainable. The Divine Father placed Himself in His Divine Son in order to become accessible to humans. All the fullness of the Divine Father dwells in the Divine Son (Colossians 1:19; 2:9) and is expressed through the Divine Son (John 1:18).

The Divine Son, the Word of Divinity (John 1:1) incarnate, is visible and accessible. Humans can see the Divine Father, touch Him, and have communion with Him through the Divine Son.

The first stage of Divinity dispensing itself to humans is through the corporification and incarnation of Himself in the Divine Son as man, thus reproducing Himself in humans.

The second stage of Divinity dispensing itself to humans is through the incarnate Divine Son. Christ is the corporification of Divinity. Through His incarnation, the Divine Son brought Divinity to humans and blended the divine nature with human nature. Christ lived on Earth for thirty-three years and experienced daily human life. Christ entered death and passed through it, freeing humans from it. After the resurrection, Christ did not shed His humanity; Christ continues to be both human and divine. By His ascension to heaven, Christ is above all. Christ, the human with a divine nature, is enthroned in heaven as the Head of the universe.

The third stage of Divinity dispensing itself to humans is that both the Divine Father and the Divine Son are in the Divine Spirit. Everything that is in the Divine Father is in the Divine Son, and both, the Divine Father and the Divine Son, containing all elements in Christ, are introduced into the Divine Spirit (2 Corinthians 3:17; John 4:24).

The Divine Spirit has the divine nature and all the elements of the human nature of Christ, and as such, this all-inclusive Divine Spirit came into humans and upon humans. The Divine Spirit is in humans, and human nature is in Him.

Christ is the expressed divinity, and the Divine Spirit is Christ perceived in reality. When the Divine Spirit enters into humans, then divinity is dispensed to the spirit of the human being.

The human person is an integrated body and soul.

A human person is both a bodily and a spiritual being. A human person is a spiritual being because their body is animated by a principle of spiritual life called the soul. The human body (material) united with the human soul (spiritual) forms a single human nature. The soul is created by the Divine at the exact moment of human conception. The Integral Person (body and soul) comes into existence at the moment of conception by the biological parents.

The vision you adopt for anthropology affects how you experience Christianity. The individual human being is a substantial unity with multiple dimensions. What happens to the individual human being impacts all their dimensions.

The models used to describe the individual human being are:

1) Monism: a single element in the human being. Monism asserts that human nature is indivisible. The Human Being

should not be perceived as composed of "parts" but rather, the Human Being is a unity, a "self."

2) Dichotomy: two elements in one being. The human being formed by a material element (the body) and a spiritual element (the soul).

3) Trichotomy: three elements in one being. The human being formed by a material element (the body, 'basar' in Hebrew, 'soma' in Greek); a psychological element (the soul, 'nephesh' in Hebrew, 'psuche' in Greek); a religious element (the spirit, 'ruach' in Hebrew, 'pneuma' in Greek).

4) Multidimensional: multiple dimensions in one being. The human being formed by the personal (I) dimension; emotional; psychic; historical; social; cosmic; material; etc.

The human being only exists in their entirety; that is, one element without the others does not represent the integral human being. Our entire being—our intellect, our will, our emotions, our intuition—are all involved in our knowledge of the Divine. The Divine does not relate to the human being in fragmented terms, but the whole person of the human being is important to the Divine.

Regarding the biblical citations 2 Corinthians 5:8 and Matthew 10:28, and others that indicate that, in death, the immaterial part leaves the body, Joseph Ratzinger explains that "the soul is a notion that expresses the personal unity of man as a supramaterial being."

According to Joseph Ratzinger in *Sacramentum Mundi*, volume 4, p. 399:

"... every statement about body and soul... always aims at the one man, but within his internally differentiated state of a principle of spiritual and material being, that is to say, of a being that equally participates in the spiritual dimension and in the dimension of space and time. – The two statements cannot refer to two distinct beings, but they cannot be simply identified either. This also holds true with respect to the statement about the fulfillment of soul and body. The expression that speaks of an intermediate state of soul without a body, 'before' the resurrection of the body, does not want (theologically read) to fix anything, except for the necessary differentiation of the two statements. Only together do they truly define the being of man and its fulfillment."

The human being is both material and immaterial, but the Divine is interested in the human being as a whole. The overall emphasis of the Bible is that the Divine is concerned with every facet of the human being, and that there is no aspect of a human being's life that is outside the Love and Divine Providence.

According to W. Pannenberg, *Was ist der Mensch?* (What is Man?), Göttingen, 1981, p. 36:

"The human being does not possess a soul as an independent reality, in opposition to the body itself; nor does it possess a body that moves in a completely mechanical or unconscious manner. Both ideas are abstractions. What really exists is the unity of the living being, the human person who moves and reacts to the world."

According to Giovanni Ancona; *Christian Eschatology*, Loyola Editions, 2013, p. 313

"The resurrection, in other words, is the event that fulfills man in his substantial unity of body and soul that personally identifies him; thus, when we affirm the reunification of the soul with the body in the resurrection, we do not mean the act of recomposing two separated entities, but the realization of human identity in the totality of its spiritual and corporeal expressions."

According to J. L. Ruiz De La Peña, *L'altra dimensione, Christian Eschatology*, Rome, Borla, 1981, p. 218

"The body is the totality of the unified man that presents itself externally, as the soul is the same undivided totality in its interiority and depth."

Everything that happens to the human person happens to this integral person.

……………………………………

The totality of the person is body, soul, and spirit.

Extracted from the text "The Function of the Mantra" from the series of lectures given by D. Bede Griffiths – OSB at the John Main Seminar in 1991.

For meditation, the body and mind need to be completely relaxed so that the spirit can be fully open and receptive to the Holy Spirit of Divinity.

Brother Angelino, in his prayer before Christian meditation, asks that the Holy Spirit of Divinity relax the body, calm the mind, and soothe the heart.

The mantra serves to recompose the soul, bringing it back to its center, and uniting the totality of the person (body, soul, and spirit) with the Holy Spirit of Divinity.

The totality of the person is body, soul, and spirit:

We have a body, the physical organism that connects us to all physical organisms in the universe.

We have a soul, the psyche, which is the psychological organism, with senses, feelings, imagination, reason, and will. The center of the psyche is the ego, what in Sanskrit is called *ahamkara*, the "maker of the self." The psyche is very limited.

But beyond it, there is the spirit, the *Atman*, which is the point of transcendence of the self. At that point, body and soul go beyond their human limitations, opening up to the infinite, the eternal, the divine.

Meditation is the passage beyond the body and soul, to that point of the spirit.

The goal of meditation is to center the body and soul in the depths of the spirit, where the human spirit meets the Spirit of Divinity.

At that point of the spirit, we transcend the ego and open ourselves to the Holy Spirit. It is a meeting point for our spirit and the Spirit of Divinity.

Meditation should be that meeting point, where the human spirit touches and opens to the Holy Spirit of Divinity. It is interesting how the word "spirit" is sometimes used in the New Testament for the human, and other times for the divine: because it is the meeting point. The spirit is what St. Francis de Sales called "the refined point of the soul." It is the point of transcendence of the self, from where we go beyond ourselves and receive the divine Holy Spirit in our hearts, that is, to the center of our being. The repetition of the mantra is a simple way to keep all the faculties of the soul and body centered on that point of the spirit.

For the Christian, the point of the spirit is the point where the love of Divinity floods the heart through the Holy Spirit.

....

Extracted from the text "The Love That Divinizes" on pages 73 to 77 of the book "The Light That Comes from Within" by Laurence Freeman.

Meditation leads us to achieve awareness of the meaning of the word "spirit." According to the perspective of Father John Main, the primary purpose of the silence of meditation is to allow us to find our own spirit. As we become quieter, we also become more aware of what spirit is, as we more consciously awaken to the dimension of our being.

We understand that the spirit is contained in a dimension that differs from both the mind and the body, that the spirit is not located well within the body, like a ghost in a machine, nor exactly in the mind; although it is situated above space, it is more like a mysterious point where body and mind unite and transcend in their activity or process.

As Saint Paul taught, the spiritual is our immortal part; it is the infinite point that absorbs the mortal and the finite. It is in the spirit that body and mind come together. The discovery of the spirit is a work of integration and harmonization that we feel intensifying through meditation.

We ask ourselves, "What is the spirit?" and we find it increasingly difficult to find the answer. It would be easier to respond if it were possible to establish a clear opposition between the different aspects of our being, which are the aspects we deal with in our daily life, in our relationships, and in our reflections on the mystery of life: the dimensions of body, mind, and spirit.

As we progress on the journey of meditation, we realize over time that we cannot make definitive oppositions between these three dimensions (body, mind, and spirit) because, through the discovery of the spirit, we become more rooted, more real in the other two dimensions as well.

To ask, "What is the spirit?" is to ask, "Who am I?" This question is the simplest of all and can only be answered by knowing that "I am the person who is asking the question."

The spirit is the basic and radically simple identity of what we are, the most irreducible aspect of the person we are, the person that Divinity knows and loves. The spirit encompasses mind and body and each dimension of our life, and it leads all these dimensions to the realization of their full potential when we can allow the spirit to act freely. The function of meditation would therefore be this: to learn to be.

This is also the function of the silence of meditation, in which we allow consciousness to travel naturally to its exact starting point. This point is the center of our being, where we find ourselves close to Divinity, where we come into harmony with ourselves and with the Spirit of Divinity.

About the Author

Décio Martins de Medeiros has published books on poetry, theology, religion, management, sales, genealogy, memoirs, and entertainment. He participates in the blog Prazer Compartilhar and the Clube de Autores.

The covers and synopses of his books are presented at:

https://sites.google.com/view/autordeciomartinsdemedeiros/

Divinity and electricity

www.ingramcontent.com/pod-product-compliance
Lightning Source LLC
LaVergne TN
LVHW010119170826
845678LV00012B/2499

* 9 7 9 8 2 3 0 2 1 2 6 0 7 *